Edge of Forever

Jeannette Isabella

Edge of Forever

Jeannette Isabella

TransMedia Press
Philadelphia, PA

Photos/Illustration

Monument to Harriet Tubman, Page 13
Billie Holiday, Page 21
Jazz Trio, Page 25

Edge of Forever / Jeannette Isabella — 1st ed.

ISBN 978-0-9820255-0-5

TransMedia Press is an imprint of
The TransMedia Publishing Group

Dedication

To my beloved family and the angels
who have sheltered me under their wings

Epigraph

"In recognizing the humanity of our fellow beings, we pay ourselves the highest tribute."

Thurgood Marshall

Acknowledgements

Sweet spirit joy and uncloudy blue sky gratitude to:

- *My beautiful, amazing, talented family, the starlight of my existence, my explanation for everything. Thank you for your unwavering support, unconditional love and understanding. I love you. This one's for you!*

- *Benson Fishman for using his tremendous talents and expertise to guide this work from a misty dream to reality. We did it, B!*

- *The members of the Poetry Workshop at Olli/Temple University, facilitated by Professor Emeritus Alison Tasch. Thank you for your invaluable insights and advice. Write on!*

- *My friends who encouraged my work and patiently asked "Where is the book, J?" Thank you for your faith in me. Consider it done!*

Contents

Mists

We are but time's dusty nomads, brief wayfarers

sojourning in shadows, then passing away

Yet on this mortal journey

our solitary footsteps across life's rocky paths

ignite sparks that streak across twilight of heaven

and cause even angels to pause

৵৵৵

The Journey

Lucifer

fallen Angel of Deception

sought mortal corruption so foul

God

would surely turn away from man

and man

abandoned

forever forsaken

forever forgotten

forever bereft of joy

forever despaired of hope

forever lost from love

would curse God

fall

become Hell's chattel

forevermore

So Lucifer, certain as sin

turned his quest

to human realms of being

Crawled catacombs of mortal souls

courted man's vilest abominations

seduced spirits of fear, hate

incited treachery, greed

quickened demons of war

murder, rape, torture

Then pregnant with horrors of hell

spawned endless bondage

christened his serpent

slavery

So shadowed under the hand of the Evil One

so man defiled his first home

So man stole land

so man stole diamonds

so by gold possessed

so man stole man

Mortals marketed as merchandise

goods bought, goods sold

Humans stripped of humanity

degraded into property

shipped as products:

loose packed, tight packed

stack packed like cordwood

on stinking vessels of torment

Justice, Liberty, Integrity...

crimsoned greedy seas

Savage slaughter so constant

sharks memorized ship's paths

forgot hunger, fattened abundant young

on floating feasts of sea-corpses

of warriors who fought to die

of miners, blacksmiths, herders, farmers

of mothers who refused to suckle slaves

of sisters, fathers, brothers, daughters

Infanticide, homicide, genocide

scores of innocents slaughtered

consumed in insatiable seas

Lucifer launched every ship

danced on every deck

rejoiced at every port

anointed every auction block

licensed every lynching

Royalty reduced to paupers

queens corrupted to concubines

artists denied, musicians silenced

scholars unschooled, cultures slaughtered

Jamestown to Appomattox

man sold man

for the land, in the land

of self evident truths

of inalienable rights

sunrise to sunset

man owned man

Idle practitioners of pale, false civilities

arrogant heirs of putrid, peculiar institutions

preached doctrines of domination, nullification

Partus sequitur ventrem

blood to blood to blood

enslaved descendants scourged with maternal bondage

so bonded mothers bore bonded sons

bonded mothers bore boded daughters

free fathers sired bonded sons

free fathers sired bonded daughters

free brothers owned bonded sisters

free sisters owned bonded brothers

Miscegenation, degradation, subjugation, brutalization

generation, after generation, after generation

But amid thunderous terror

roaring avarice, exploding evils

a slave's silent prayer to Heaven

caused Lucifer to pause

What if least of these

became greatest of these?

What if last became first

when forced to their knees in crushing tribulation

humanity denied, souls seared

stripped of hope, bereft of joy

yet still ascended in faith

and clenched immutable truth:

Fortunes fall, kingdoms fade

man's destiny determined not

by temporal possessions mortal hands grasp

but by eternal treasures immortal hearts embrace

So lest agony of enslavement cease

still rage of the murdering lash

arouse mercies in money-maddened minds

extinguish fires of branding irons

release chokeholds of lynch ropes

silence screams at auction blocks

Lucifer, Great Deceiver

Lucifer, Great Liar

counseled Kingdoms of Cotton

of Indigo, Sugarcane, Rice, Tobacco

"They are beings of inferior order

and have no rights

you are bound to respect

Is not your wealth

sign of Heaven's grace?

Let the circle be unbroken

let the chains remain

let your will be done"

Then Angel of Evil lifted the veil

turned to Heaven

exposed demonic greed, arrogant abominations

unholy horrors, vile affronts to God

and loudly mocked:

"Behold Your Children!"

But slaves' prayers mounted wings of faith

whispers to murmurs

murmurs to shouts

shouts to screams soared

until Cavalry cries of captive ones

pierced celestial side and Heaven debated:

"May mortal man undo

labors of an Angel?"

From edge of forever

God

composer of cosmos

author of infinity

creator of angels

heaven, earth and men

charged with thunderous coldfire:

"Moses Once, Moses Twice".

In Dorchester County

He spoke to one

body bound, spirit free

God's property forever

Harriet heard His voice

answered His command:

"Lead my people free!"

God opened up windows of Heaven

poured Harriet starshine north

from manacles of Maryland

to refuge of Philadelphia, Canada-bound

Fleeting daymoon repose followed

long starlight flight

Bounty heavy on her head

patrollers sniping at her back

bloodhound law howling at her heels

But darker the night

the brighter His light

So Harriet walked and walked and walked

She walked

plunged rag-bound, frosted feet

into icy, crusted Christmas snow

She walked

unshakeable, with faint-hearted through woods

"Hears dogs, Ms Harriet, I can't, the dogs"

"I said I leaves nobody behind alive!"

She walked

while reassuring homesick sisters:

"I comes back next time for your brothers"

She walked

while comforting anxious elders

"You're gonna rest soon on free land"

She walked with fathers

so freed fathers could stand tall in eyes of sons

She walked with sons

so freed sons could be the men their fathers dreamed

She walked with daughters

so freed daughters could be the women their mothers dreamed

She walked with mothers

so freed mothers could raise free sons

so freed mothers could raise free daughters

She walked

hunted, hidden, hounded, hungry

secret knocks, whispered codes

"A friend with friends"

She walked

ninety miles circled nineteen times

three hundred captives unbound

And then she walked

unstoppable

stormed crowded courtroom

so Nalle could flee away

She walked

aboard Union gunboats on Combahee

engineered jubilee of over seven hundred and fifty

She walked

so scholars could once again discover

so teachers could once again inspire

so poets could once again sing

Never alone and always alone

through hell's ecstasy, heaven's sorrows

through the valley of the shadow of death

Harriet walked with God

And when her journey ended

her "ordie" over

just Jordan's River left to cross

Angel Gabriel lifted weary feet

Araminta Harriet Ross Tubman Davis

flew away free

forevermore

Meanwhile, outside Time

Lucifer turned round

to human realms of being

again

❧ ❧

Rhythms for Harriet Tubman's Journey

What's that howl, Harriet, worrying midnight air?

Beware, Harriet, beware

Could that sound be hounds of hell, trying to halt those freedom bound?

Come 'round here, Lord, come 'round

What's that star, Harriet, glistening in Christmas skies?

Shine on, shine down until morn

Must be light to guide you on, keep you safe 'til dawn

Hold on Harriet, hold on

What's that storm cloud, Harriet, gathering across the sky?

Must be John Brown's shadow, passing by and by

What's that thunder, Harriet, roaring across the land?

Sound of bondage chained to blood, civil war at hand

Walk on, Harriet, walk on, freedom's sun will rise

Appomattox Courthouse, 1865

Your walk of courage will come to be

the walk of those who yearn for liberty

❧

Harriet Tubman: Life Celebrated As Heroic Art

"Every great dream begins with a dreamer. Always remember, you have within you the strength, the patience, and the passion to reach for the stars to change the world"

Harriet Tubman

Monument to Harriet Tubman and the Underground Railroad in Boston, MA

Born enslaved in Dorchester County, Maryland around 1820, Araminta Harriet Ross Tubman Davis's life was a portrait in courage, determination and strength. Beginning with her self-emancipation in 1849, the lionhearted Ms Tubman plunged over and over again into the abyss of slavery to boldly rescue hundreds of persons while endangering her own freedom. She braved numerous grueling journeys (which she referred to as "the ordie") into Maryland to liberate relatives and friends. In April of 1860, in direct defiance of the Fugitive Slave Act, Ms Tubman stormed into a Troy, New York Commissioner's office and snatched runaway slave Charles Nalle from his captors. Ms Tubman safely delivered Nalle to the waiting arms of a local group of abolitionists known as the Vigilance Committee. In June of 1863, Ms Tubman journeyed into South Carolina Low Country. She, along with Colonel James Montgomery, led the successful Combahee River raid, which resulted in the liberation of over seven hundred and fifty people. Many of the freed slaves joined the Union Army. With her unwavering faith in God as her canvas, Ms Tubman painted a life story of uncommon bravery and sacrifice, sculpted in compassion, written in blood, sweat and tears.

J.I.

Dreams Denied

Young Jamaal won't be home for dinner tonight

his small room gravely silent

no raucous boyish games invade his shroud laid domain

And his mother still sets his place at the table

and his father works harder than ever before

and his sister sits alone at her bedroom window

and his dog still lies by the bolted front door

But Jamaal won't be home for dinner tonight

Violence destroys dreams love cannot restore

Death stood sentry at corners

of perilous grounds on that gray November day

as young Jamaal, happily bouncing his basketball

ventured out to the street corner to play

When suddenly whirlwinds of fatal madness

rampaged angry air with deadly intent

bullets savaged Jamaal's soft ten-year-old heart

warm life flooded cold slabs of cement

Scholarly coalitions pronounced community afflictions

acute poverty and chronic drug addictions

Foul forces inferred young victim's skin

night stained hue of inherited sin

Marauding agents of chaos escalated urban rages

invading drugs enslaved fools and sages

warring guns fired graves with new and aged

Tech 9 hurricanes of hollow point bullets and white robed cocaine stormed places where no munitions factories or poppy fields reigned

So bitter the claims, so murderous the shame

so many perished, numbers erased names

And neither wars, wonders, preachers or politicians

theories, tears, prayers or skilled physicians

would save an innocent lost at play

So now Jamaal's sorrowed mother cradles her sleeping son

in hallows of a fractured mind will alone cannot mend

Yesterday's dream entombed in grave despair

she prays for deliverance to uncloudy amen

And Jamaal's father labors long for family flight to fairer soil

binds spirit wounds left by dream's untimely end

in cruel chains of weighty toil

As selfsame evil that waylaid destiny

slowly slays his anguished soul

troubled heart one year left to be

tortured center will no longer hold

And Jamaal's sister mourns in secret isolation

perfect smiles, perfect grades shade perfect desperation

As haunted by sweet dreams of her brother in happier days

anorexia fattened by grief's devastation

steadily spirits fading flesh away

And valleys give rise to mountains

And streams to rivers to oceans recall

Life of the great tethered forever to the least

Death of the tall starts with the small, envelopes all

Young Jamaal won't be home for dinner tonight.

☙❧

Around Philly Towne

Up Philly Towne, rivers run red

young blood red, innocence shed

Children play under watchful eyes

for many died as bullets blazed by

So newly quick, so quickly dead

Up Philly Towne

Dreams locked down, hopes unsaid

the least struggle the most for bread

Prayers and politicians fail to answer why

hunger haunts, murders multiply

Up Philly Towne

Down Philly Towne

crown jewel of urban high-brow

center of city power and corporate dollars

Luxury high rise towers, overshadow

cardboard boxes where homeless cower

Down Philly Towne

wealth and influence intertwine

define, dismiss, divide, deny

as innocents die, as poverty intensifies

as angels cry, as red rivers multiply

Up and Down Philly Towne

❧

Spring Scenes on Kelly Drive

Sitting in Saturday sunshine on stone footed bench
I am lost in novella's spell, kindled in quiet repose
hoping to escape chaotic rush of city life
On abandoned, dusty fountain
an ambitious spider busily weaves her deadly artistry
While nearby, four Canada geese raucously bodyguard
seven reluctant goslings to Schuylkill's edge
Weekend athletes speed furiously along;
sweat robed runners crowned with haloes of buzzing gnats
engaged in circular races to go nowhere fast
Waves of honking bicyclists whiz by shouting "Behind you"
Diminutive dog walker struggles to control
two barking rottweilers, both eager to run in opposing directions
Four laughing teenagers thunderously skateboard by
as an unhappy driver loudly disputes
to no one in particular, his newly acquired parking ticket
Air all around a raucous river of urban uproar
hotspot of perpetual motion , abuse of peaceful contemplation
Suddenly, from across the frenzied pathway,
a painter waves, lifts a blue tinged brush of life,
a silent salute to joy of creativity
I raise my book in a toast to imagination
And as lilac scents softly whisper
on sweet breezes from nearby flowering shrubs,
I exhale.

Blues Absolute

Went down to deep, Blue River

told Old Blue River my man and I were through

Stared down old, cold river bottom

cried "Blue River, that man and I are through"

Blue River roared "Get off my banks, woman

'fore I end up jumpin' into you"

Ask me a mean, cold color

believe I'll answer blue

Go on now, ask me to name some mean, cold colors

believe I'll cry the blues

Mean cold blues stay on my mind

since you up and left without a clue

Somebody stole Big Mama's hound dog

snatched her ball and chain too

What'd you say?

Some fool done stole Big Mama's howlin' hound dog

ran off with her ball and chain too

Big Mama died boardin' house down, whiskey hard times blue

chitlin' circuit tired, friends so few

Ask me a mean, cold color

I'll sing you a song in the key of blue

Wanna hear some mean, cold colors?

Sit down; take a listen to "Big Mama's Blues"

Mean cold blues will leave you hungry

lonely and tired too

Mean Mississippi back roads

sure can shake your faith away

Sing it again now

Mean Mississippi back roads

sure can shake your faith away

Cold death baptized Bessie's blues at Clarksdale

downhearted troubles sanctified at her grave

Ask me a mean cold color

believe I'll call code blue

Wanna travel to cold colorline country

get a mean front seat view?

Drive down Jim Crow's rutted roads

stop at crossroads of Abandoned and Blue

That's where mighty blues sisters are silenced forever

and never, never come back home to you

Angel of Harlem

ridin' dragon, singin' evil blues

Listen here now: Sweet Angel of Harlem

singin' blood stained "Strange Fruit" blues

She told old, cold tambourine man

"tain't nobody's business if I do"

Ask me a mean, cold color

then watch the world turn deadly blue

Go on now, just ask about mean, cold colors

I'm gonna testify to Billie's blues

High cold blues lynched Lady's Day's tomorrows

snuffed out her lost yesterdays, too

Sittin' alone in this juke joint

drinkin' moonshine, listenin' to down home blues

I'm tellin' you, I'm sittin' here in this funky juke joint

tears saltin' my whisky, moanin' to low down, dirty blues

Those crazy blues got me feelin' real mellow

lyin', swearin', I ain't missing you.

So ask me how to find those mean, cold colors

I'll tell you tonight I'm goin' home with Mister Blues

And first thing tomorrow morning

stone cold sober Blues is gonna shake me, wake me,

hold me, rock me, take me like you useta do

❧❧

Blues Absolute Notes

I wrote Blues Absolute in response to a challenge to create a poem about a color. I decided to center the poem on my favorite color, blue and incorporate a blues-like quality to the work. Blues Absolute features three female African American musical artists of unparalleled talents: Big Mama Thornton, Bessie Smith and Billie Holiday.

Big Mama Thornton was born on December 11, 1926 in Ariton Alabama. She was a blues singer and song writer who recorded (and by some accounts wrote) *Hound Dog* before Elvis Presley's massive hit. Big Mama also wrote and recorded *Ball and Chain* prior to Janis Joplin's huge 1960's version. Big Mama Thornton died penniless, in a boarding house on July 25, 1984, the same year she was inducted into the Blues Hall of Fame.

Billie "Lady Day" Holiday

Bessie Smith, born April 15, 1894 was called the Empress of the Blues. Bessie Smith was the most popular blues singer of the 1920's and 1930's. Her recording of *Downhearted Blues* was included in the list of Songs of the Century by the Recording Industry of America and the National Endowment for the Arts in 2001. *Downhearted Blues* is in the Rock and Roll Hall of Fame as one of the five hundred songs that shaped modern rock n roll. Bessie Smith died on September 26, 1937 at the age of 43 after being involved in a tragic automobile accident just outside Clarksdale, Mississippi. The quality and degree of her medical care has been a source of great consternation and controversy. Smith's funeral was held in Philadelphia where over 10,000 mourners paid respects. Her grave remained unmarked until a tombstone paid for by Janis Joplin was erected.

The incomparable Billie "Lady Day" Holiday, composer and singer, born April 7, 1915, was also known as the "Angel of Harlem." Her vocal style was a seminal influence on jazz and pop artists. Ill and addicted to heroin, Billie Holiday was taken to Metropolitan Hospital in NY where she was arrested for drug possession. As she lay dying, she was handcuffed to her bed and her hospital room was raided by authorities. Progressively swindled out of her earnings, she died on July 17, 1959 with seventy cents in the bank. Riding the dragon refers to a heroin induced high and tambourine man was a code name for the drug dealer. Strange Fruit is an iconic song penned by poet and social activist Abel Meeropol about the horrors of lynching and racism. Ms Holiday began performing *Strange Fruit* at every concert as her signature closing song. In 1999, Time Magazine named Billie Holiday's first studio version of *Strange Fruit* the "Song of the Century."

J.I.

Deep River Blues

Alone, wearing a tattered, soiled bridal gown

she gathered up her scattered sorrows

and under a barren tree by the deep river she lay down

"I am cursed by love" she confessed to twilight skies above

"So, I will drown my tomorrows in this river of unrequited love"

When suddenly, catty corner to rising quarter moon

whistling an off key tune

wearing a pink tutu and rhinestone speckled green

and purple polka dot shoes

a gnome-like being of mysterious identity appeared

Fading sunlight glistened and sparkled around the creature as it asked

"Pretty lady, why the blues?"

Startled at first, then comforted by concern for her dismay

she spoke longingly to the creature about past romances gone astray

"Many times I thought happiness was mine

but time revealed true love was not to come my way

So I will wear this wedding gown

and live alone on the riverbank until my dying day"

The creature delicately replied

"Living alone by this river will be many years of fears and tears

If you can't find love with someone else

why not simply love yourself?"

"Who are you?"

she asked after realizing the creature's advice was wise and true

"I am your creativity and your hope

I am the laughter and joy you once knew

I am you

Take my hand, come join with me

Celebrate, rejoice in life and be free to happily be"

So together they left after casting into the deep river

all her woes and all her blues

And the trees and the breeze heard her ask

"Where did you get those gorgeous shoes?"

❧❧

The Turnaround

Gray tweed devotee of rationality was he

overcast by should, chained to ought to be

Led uptight days of regimented black-white rigidity

yet midnight dreamed of letting loose, flying free

Golden blue note jazz spirit she

soul tripping on cool side of quarter moon reverie

purple funk in fusion air, electric vibes everywhere

swinging, be bopping on Blue Train to Saint Coltrane jubilee

He heard her improv a score halfway to Heaven's door

while on musical quest to cast off convention

enticed by syncopation, seduced by harmony, he found redemption

discovered jubilation in her charms, got an education in her arms

Now his groove is tight, his rhythms out of sight and free

released inhibitions, embraced creativity

plays pizzicato bass fiddle at jam sessions, to her delight

together they make love with music all through the night

❦

Saturday Night at the Blue Note Jazz Club

Blue tipplers drifting

on smoky blue tunes

Blues singer mourning

fleeting blue serene

Blues sax crying

bitter blue croon

Blue notes wailing

under June blue moon

Crossings

Chincoteague causeway at eventide

meandering highway balanced on bay

where blue skies ribbon marsh-rimmed seas

At Cockle's Creek, below the road

a solitary great blue heron wades across sandy shores

Overhead, calls of laughing gulls pierce autumn air

and turkey vultures circle, circle, waiting to feast

on victims of the indifferent road

Streamers of snow geese, Assateague Island bound

loudly migrate through cloudless skies

Calm seas and sweet winds almost lull the senses into believing

Ash Wednesday '62 merely stormy memory

and September serenity will last forever

And legends whisper that in dying light, just at water's edge

shadows of aboriginal Assateagues can sometimes be seen

silently fishing along mist shrouded shores

until swallowed by nightfall of eternity

❧❧

Why Change

So thin

she almost wasn't there

startled hair woven like

abandoned pigeon's nest

soiled spider arms

cobwebbed with elusive dreams

yesterday's debaucheries

still dancing round her

she shoelessly slumped

against unyielding brick wall

raised untouchable palms skyward

as if in search of rain or manna

"Can you spare some change?"

I stopped and wondered

why change

was always

so hard to come by?

❧❧

The Hunger

Sometimes

not second sight of learned seers

nor wisdom gleaned from yesterday's tears

nor pained recall of love's depart

can quell unyielding longing

of a disobedient heart

❧

Illusions

Reality turns out to be

what it's not supposed to be

and before you realize it

there it is

Not.

❧

An Exhausted Sanitation Worker's
Hands to Heaven
Anguished Lament To God
On A Searing Hot And
Humid Late August Afternoon

"Why Flies?????"

Judgement Day

Listen, listen, listen

heard what doomdayers say?

Someday soon, in a most unhappy way

could be tomorrow, perhaps today

Listen, listen, listen

some now say

Swiftly comes end of days.

Water, water everywhere

melting polar caps flood undone

thunderclouds deny the sun

Water, water everywhere

oceans roam capsized roads

seas shroud desert shores

Water, water everywhere

terra firma is no more.

Listen, listen, listen

hear horsemen ride, ride, ride ride?

chaos, unholy destruction, global homicide

Scholars of international diplomatic persuasion

foresee Armageddon as global nuclear conflagration

Military conflicts speedily escalate, countdowns zero end

first two fission driven war heads cross paths

then four, suddenly ten

Mushroom clouds overshadow city after city

mass destruction descends

vaporizing heat becomes death's newest protégé

Then invading nuclear winter enters battle fray

imprisons wounded planet with impregnable glacial overlay

Humanity undone, all born of woman become vanquished prey

of blood red "U235 fire this time" betray.

Or could humanity cease in a celestial way

as corrupt renegade comet ends our days

Icy great rock goes murderously astray

abandons ancient path, into Earth's orbit strays

Plunges straight into planet's watery heart

cosmic collision almost shears Earth apart

ejected debris seals off Sun's rays

impenetrable darkness obliterates light of day

volcanoes scream, earthquakes roar, continents, rise, fall, sway

The cake and the bones of humanity swiftly passes away.

Listen, listen listen

what's that they say?

Could be tomorrow, maybe today

Is it possible civilization could end this way?

Some fear our sun in zenith

will solar storm slay

as violent orgasmic ejection

of highly charged protons explode Earth's way

Annihilating X class solar flares discharge fatal day

satellites, cell phones useless, transformers fried planet wide

Total loss of electronic power unleashes global uproar

food, clean water spun into gold, commodity prices soar

Pestilence, starvation devour humanity as never before

riots, political upheavals, terror, terror, terror

War, war and more war

Soon fragile civilization will exist no more.

Now you've listened

heard what doomdayers say

Something wicked this way comes

from sky, from fire, from water, from sun

Someday soon to those fashioned of clay

could be tomorrow, maybe today

Earth and heaven will all pass away

Swiftly comes end of days.

❧

Tourists

Asteroid 1998QE2 flew into blue Earth's view

dragged along a moonlet friend for cosmic ride two

Astronomers gazed up at occupied skies, identified

approaching Amor sooty asteroid as over a mile wide

NASA got excited, staged "Meet the Geeks show"

supplied technical facts for starry-eyed to know

reassured press and public there was nothing to fear

but doomsayers predicted Earth's end was near

And 1998 QE2 whizzed by with a 3 million mile sway

hauling its old friend in tow and streaked harmlessly away

৵৻৵

It's Getting Hot in Here

Earth's got greenhouse fever

snow covers melting down

glaciers retreating, ice sheets shrinking

oceans heating, mercury's on the rise

Meteorological despair everywhere

as super storms ram into town.

Scientists warn:

"Stop deforestation" "Burn less fossil fuels"

Because Earth has greenhouse fever

her temperature soars and soars

cities frying, forests drying, species dying

sea levels rising, flooding on coastal shores

nature's fury released on a massive score

The heat is on; Earth's fever must be cured

before humanity becomes as extinct as dinosaurs

❧❦

I Hope I Shall Never See
The Day A.I. Overwrites Humanity

Scientists warn at the current tech pace

Artificial Intelligence could soon eclipse the human race

Flesh and blood control would fade away

bots and data would command the day

What sort of world would A.I. create?

Will resistance be futile and termination our fate?

Or will mortals and machines someday marry

and cyborgs become people extraordinary?

And if A.I. should ever make a tree

what kind of God would A.I. be?

❧❧

A Ballade of Delay

The challenge to write a poem seemed fine
but attempts to create quickly ended
distractions began before my first line
Procrastination pays no dividends
yet still I delayed, had e-mail to send
turned to laptop for online shopping spree
garden needed tending, spread mulch 'round trees
My hectic day flew swiftly away
muse, unfortunately, an absentee
and I did not write a poem that day

Yesterday, old friends came at noon to dine
held debates on movies to recommend.
A few moments to watch TV, unwind
off to post office, packages to send
Stopped by an ATM for cash to spend
on to store, picked up latest DVD
toothpaste and milk, small box of Earl Gray tea
Home in comfy chair, read book on Monet
fell asleep, dreamed water lilies, blue seas
and I did not write a poem that day

But time cares not for a wandering mind
days rush to seasons and rapidly end
Seduced by moments, I became inclined
to scatter hours as my days unbend
Suddenly Reason urged, "Carpe Diem!"
Brief Life carries no end date guarantees
and there will never be another me
to simply sing my soul's passions my way
So from procrastination, I'll break free
and I'll live my finest poem this day

۞

Jilted

Not so long ago, we soared together

wild, free words winged

across clean, smooth pages

like homebound eagles

against sea merged sky

We were one

But clouds came between us

You abandoned me

Alone, I crashed.

From daymoon's rise to twilight's fall

I called to you

You would not respond.

I staked out our library

wanting to waylay you

in familiar surroundings

You stayed away.

My bright red convertible pen

drove around bonded paper

hoping you'd ask for a ride

Bought a new dictionary

borrowed an expensive thesaurus

You were not impressed.

Shopping around in my mind for hours

tried on tight adjectives

come hither verbs

scandalous nouns

You were not aroused.

So today I stood

before the altar

of an impatient audience

without you

Speechless.

❧

Scheherazade's Rap

Impossible to understand
easy to love
despite capricious demands
often displaying circular gyrations
of opposing sensations
alternating torrents of affection
with stone wall rejections
Scheherazade
green eyed, have at, tit for tat, tabby cat
now fitfully naps
Are her sporadic devotions
sincere emotions
or ploys she joyously employs
to obtain treats and catnip filled toys?
Who knows
if her noonday doze
is merely brief repose
before midnight terror patrols
unroll my sleep and bedclothes?
Oh no!
Still, I suppose
I could have chose
a laid back, no attack
sweetly purring pussycat
some mellow, yellowfellow chap
content to calmly nap in my lap
no nocturnal prowls
no demanding meows
no early morning blue howls
Yet, if she could yackety-yak
Scheherazade
would rapidly red rap back
"Where's the fun in all that
Jack?"

ৡৢ

Memories

Alone
I'll remember you
as spring and robins marry
on sweet blue sky days
on young May mornings
on ruby kissed dawns
Alone
I'll remember our together
with free flowing memories
with arrested tears
Alone
I'll remember our parting
one torn from two
forever divided from you
Alone
I'll remember
all our yesterdays
for all my tomorrows
And grateful for mortal fragility
I'll briefly bear
your unbearable leaving
and ponder immortal
solitude of God
who remembers
all our tears
all our fears
all our days
all eternity
Alone

Resurrection

I've been here before

spirit captive in carbon cage

soul subdued to fleshly ways

hostage to sorrow and joy, youth and age

Until the time, when out of time

in mortal night, Death has its day

and debt to life paid once again

to undiscovered country, I'll fly away

And wait for time when there is no time

when yesterday, today, tomorrow, are no more

I'll refuse an Earthly encore, be spirit forevermore

for I've been here before

❧

Rule of Rapture

Love, square root of joy

Multiplies when divided

Subtracts fear, adds peace

❧

Night Dreams

Last night I dreamed of freshly baked, buttermilk bread

warm, crusty slabs , smothered in grape jelly spread

I dreamed of flaky croissants, filled with melted dark chocolate shreds

of soft floured biscuits, shining with strawberry jam, freckled red

Last night I dreamed of bread

Last night I dreamed of children dancing, gloriously at play

healthy children in cities large, rural towns small, hunger held at bay

poverty defeated, starvation no longer shrouds tender days

I dreamed of all the world's children, happy, strong, well fed

Last night I dreamed of bread

✧✧

Sociopath's Song

(Opus Ruthless Dissonance:
Performed in the Key of Mean Sharp)

Common, ordinary murder is unappealing

a nasty situation to wisely evade

Grimy, smelly bodily fluids, slimy disgusting bloodstains

detectable, pesky DNA

Vengeful relatives shrieking about retribution

expensive lawyers to be paid and paid

Loudly demanding police officers

rudely inquisitive DA's

Angry judges imposing endless sentences

to wretched cages faraway

Fleshly murder is gruesome and dirty

yet spirit slaughter is tidily clean

And no one's ever been prosecuted for being criminally mean

So if murder is your passion

but you crave staying wild and free

Forget all that bloody chaos;

rethink your basic strategy

Make tender, sweet souls your target

forget about difficult, hard bodies

First, research survival of the fittest

study nature red in tooth and claw

reverse physical to mental

Craft your victims' psychological fall

Start your spirit killing spree off right at home

by murdering family harmony

Loudly declare your quiet child stupid

whisper to your latest lover

that your loyal spouse is annoying and fat

Proclaim your despondent brother a loser

tell your ambitious sister her dreams will all fall flat

Flaunt your obvious superiority at every twist and bend

sneer at humble hardworking folks

label them and their jobs "dead-end"

Sharpen your evil tongue on a steely cold heart

hone a wicked weapon of psychological cruelty

In no time at all with practice

you'll master sadistic art of verbal inhumanity

With a few well turned phrases

you can slaughter legions of dreams and hopes

Then blame the carnage on the victims

tell them with reality they can't cope

Always wear a concerned face of reflective sincerity

so few will ever connect or suspect

And if you're ever called into question

smile as you lie and deny

just say you're being honest and direct

Sing a false song of "sticks and stones breaking bones

but words can never hurt you"

should some interfering fool cry "not fair"

While you ruthlessly criticize, falsify, justify

and multiply your harvest of cerebral despair

As long as you chose your subjects wisely

at this type of murder you can excel

And still sing in the church choir on Sunday

preach fleshly sinners straight to hell

Leave a tragic trail of emotional devastation

yet live life freely without personal dismay

You'll be welcome at the office

no hounding press will pen shocking exposés

No need for high priced attorneys

no meddlesome cops will come to call

No nosy, pushy DA's, no CSI

no embarrassing social falls

And moral retribution, with Heaven and Hell to pay

can be delayed indefinitely

until your unfortunate Judgment Day

So why bother with noisy, expensive guns

poisons are unreliable, bloody knives are grossly passé

Murder can be almost earthly risk free

when performed in a "spiritual" way.

∾৶৸

Center Stage in Her Own Mind...

performing a high wire act on red sequined, stilted shoes

wearing purple and green tutu over blue tie dyed bodysuit

she trapezed with unease across the crowded street

Chanel No 5, funk and bourbon three ringed around her

Streamers of rainbow hair waved at her fish mouthed audience

as a sideshow of corner clowns juggled questions

on where her costume ended and she began

Tears spotlighted weary flesh

through gaily painted grease paint on her face

All the while she loudly announced

over and over again:

"He'll be back tomorrow

He'll be back tomorrow"

෴

Study in Genetics

Every morning

she stands before her mirror

as her father's brown eyes

watch her mother's slim hands

brush her grandmother's curly hair

෪෨

Reflections

Fashioned in my mother's image, so our mirror recalled

Looking at her face, I learned my face

a touch of her hands graced my hands

my voice echoed her voice, my eyes revealed her eyes

But death shattered our mirror, we reflect no more

Never again to look upon her face and see my face

gone, gentle touch of her hands

her voice forever silent, her eyes forever closed

Yet God granted her memory powers that death did not destroy:

thoughts of her endless love calms my raging soul

remembering her undying devotion comforts my grieving heart

And to carry on her unconquerable joy

my mother left me her smile.

༺༻

Partners

No, Death and I cannot dance together

no grim choreographer of mortality

slowly ending jagged rhythms

of my imperfect pirouette

Yes, Life and I will embrace together

whirling, spinning, twirling

sweeping into the arms of eternity

until exhausted,

I fall

Tribute at Poet's Tomb

She's not here

She rose easily, regally

her spirit release metered metaphor

grace embellished dawn

Ascending with quiet eloquence

like sophisticated similes

Spirit soaring skyward

on seductively smooth rhythms

Dreaming done, eternity begun

gently rising inside celestial winds

prancing on dappled blue moondust

spinning between rainbowed starbeams

Free of the blood, free of the bone

airily, merrily

beckoning heaven's sweet reckoning

singing her feminine rhymes

in divine realms

of Master Artist's

ever flowing poem.

In other words

she flew away home

Listen for her lyrical legacy

in ancient ballads rebuking war

in prayerful sonnets embracing peace

in tearstained refrains of passion's retreat

Search for her verse rebirth

in whispers of spring's green promises

in lusty summer thundersongs

in bittersweet autumn's melancholy memories

in winter's shrouding frosts

Leave no tears at this tomb

She's not here

❧

www.ingramcontent.com/pod-product-compliance
Lightning Source LLC
Chambersburg PA
CBHW032154020426
42334CB00016B/1281